The Ageless Angler

A Guide to Fly Fish More as You Age

Brian Braudis

www.brianbraudis.com
www.flyfisherfitness.com

ISBN (ebook): 978-0-9971604-2-0
ISBN (paperback): 978-0-9971604-3-7

Contents

Introduction

It's true. With a shift in habits and some effort, you can fly-fish more often, with more vigor—die-hard style. I do it. Some have done it all on their own by taking their lives in a new direction. Others I have helped. Either way, our numbers are too small. Take the power of your body to heart, own it, live it, and join us. You're in good company.

The one thing many fly fishers I meet have in common is physical decline. How do I know? Because the first thing they share with me is their "specific" issue that limits their ability to fish the way they'd like—hardcore, for long stretches, in wild, remote places. The thing is, those issues aren't so specific after all: back pain, shoulder pain, stiffness, declining stamina, reduced ability to stay warm while wading (thermoregulation), and balance problems are all too common. Every fly fisher experiences them, because every fly fisher is aging.

I see it in my fishing clubs, outdoor clubs, and among friends—it's universal. Aging is the bane of all outdoor pursuits. It's frustrating because we want to stay agile, strong, and vibrant. We don't want to let a steep, rocky trail or swift current hold us back. Roadside fly-fishing is fine, but what really excites us is backpacking into remote, roadless blue-line waters.

So let me ask you directly: Do you have shoulder pain? Are you stiff when you get up from the couch or the floor? Do you get winded just putting on your waders? And do you honestly think those symptoms will improve as you age even more? You might be saying, "Symptoms? Nah, they're part of getting older." But that's old thinking. Today, we know pain, stiffness, reduced energy, loss of balance, and trouble staying warm while wading are all symptoms of aging.

And here's the real question: If you're experiencing these limits now, what do you think your body will feel like in five, ten, or twenty years? These symptoms are a built-in gift from Nature. They are early warning signs—a shot across the bow. Heads up: coasting after age forty is not neutral.

The trouble is, we're conditioned to take action only after problems show up. The medical industry reinforces this. Disease is usually diagnosed at later stages. Prevention just isn't on our medical system's radar. Doctors get paid very little—or not at all—without a firm diagnosis. Quality-of-life (healthspan) support, such as monitoring blood sugar before a diagnosis of diabetes, is typically unheard of. That's why type-2 diabetes has been called the silent killer. It festers deceptively, unmonitored behind the scenes, and is usually discovered only after advancing to one of its complications, such as high blood pressure, recurrent infections, vision changes, or kidney disease (nephropathy).

One glaring risk factor—especially for diabetes—that you will see everywhere you look is being over the age of forty-five. This should be a red flag: *look deeper, monitor me*. But it's not. "Diagnose and treat" is the dominant model. Consider this: Noah didn't start building the ark when it began to rain—he built it in anticipation. Wouldn't it be better if our medical system worked the same way, helping us anticipate and interpret the symptoms of aging, and course-correct before disease set in? But the reality is, our medical industry doesn't consider healthspan (quality of life) within its purview. That's why the word *healthcare* is a misnomer. It should be *illness care*. But I digress.

We can't rely on medical professionals to prevent disease or build our health. If we don't do it ourselves, it doesn't get done. But inattention is more common than personal initiative. Just look around and see the results.

The good news? If you learn to recognize what's happening in your body and take action, you can address the symptoms of aging before they escalate into serious disease. Here's the truth: decline associated with aging is largely lifestyle-driven. Poor lifestyle choices, extended over time, can lead to diseases that will hold you back from robust fly-fishing in your later decades. Strokes, heart attacks, high blood pressure, arthritis, diabetes, falls, fractures, and even many cancers are mostly avoidable. Being proactive beats being reactive every time.

Yet how many people do you know who are actively preparing for the inevitable changes that come with growing older? That's why we're here—to change that, one person at a time. Recognize the glaring risk factor of being over forty-five years old!

There is nothing more dangerous to us than aging. That's why many researchers view aging as a disease. In *Lifespan: Why We Age—and Why We Don't Have To*, David Sinclair, PhD, aging researcher and professor of genetics at Harvard University, writes:

"If hepatitis, kidney disease, or melanoma did the sorts of things to us that aging does, we would put those diseases on a list of the deadliest illnesses in the world. Instead, scientists call what happens to us a 'loss of resilience,' and we generally have accepted it as part of the human condition."

We are uncomfortable and do not talk about what we cannot fully understand. Sinclair is pointing to our medical industry's embarrassing and embryonic view of aging. He is saying we can and should do better than accepting—and even conceding to—aging's insidious power over us.

We must take this responsibility on ourselves. Fly-fishing with strength, vitality, and longevity depends on it. Oh, yeah, and your life depends on it too—but first things first!

A Word on Genetics

When I give talks, or in conversation, invariably genetics comes up. Some people feel saddled with bad genes. Others tell me, "I have good genes. My parents are both still alive." Researchers confirm that the genetic contribution to health and how we age amounts to about 25 percent. Relying solely on good—or less-than-stellar—inheritance is leaving too much to chance. With three-quarters of how we age determined by environmental factors, anything could happen.

I believe what it comes down to is how you want to live. Don't spin your wheels convincing yourself that doing nothing —or the bare minimum—will suffice. I don't think you're reading this book because you want to *just* live—sitting on the couch, tying flies, knitting, or playing cards.

This book is a guide to help you live the strenuous life: hiking the arduous backcountry, fly-fishing for days on end in blue-line Wilderness Areas. There are no gambles. Forget genetics and other rationalizing, and commit to living your best years as the strongest human you can be—embracing the fraction of discomfort that will give you a lifetime of vigorous fly-fishing.

Aging Is Not a Sentence to Be Endured

Aging is biological, yes—but it's also shaped by culture. And culture has filled our heads with a distorted view. The jokes, the stereotypes, the images we carry of bent-over people shuffling behind walkers or relying on carts—those aren't inevitable outcomes of aging. That's decay.

True aging is simply gray hair, wrinkles, and the gentle pull of gravity. The everyday decay we see is preventable. Getting older isn't a sentence—it's an opportunity. Aging like your parents or grandparents is not your destiny. We know more now. How you age is largely a choice.

The symptoms of aging—pain, stiffness, and fatigue—are not normal aging. They're signals from Nature, warning you that you cannot keep going like you did in your twenties and thirties and expect to thrive unconditionally. Your body has changed and requires more from you now. With new awareness and effort, you can keep fly-fishing—and doing everything else you love—with vigor well into your best years.

Older professional athletes, actors, musicians, and countless others continue to perform at high levels, not because they're rich or famous, but because they've taken charge of their health and aging. They understand they have agency. In fact, for some, making every effort to live with strength and vitality may feel less like an option and more like a responsibility.

Wealth or status is not required to do the same. You have power and capacity. It takes effort. Aging is a new landscape, and with the right care—your own "fertilizer"—the grass can be greener than ever. Approach it with awareness, effort, and intention, and aging becomes an opportunity—one that calls forth your best self. With the right approach, you build wisdom, strength, and vitality that not only maintain your fly-fishing lifestyle but elevate it.

This is especially important if you're approaching retirement. Many see this stage as a time to relax, disengage, and take it easy. But look around. Is that working for most people?

Instead of following the crowd, take the road less traveled. Retirement can be the most important health-building time of your life. The stress, time crunch, and demands of work are gone—you finally have the freedom to shape your health and future with purpose. That's *Purpose* with a capital P.

Biological Age

Chronological age—the number on the calendar—is fixed. But biological age is dynamic, and you have more control than you think. Research shows that as much as 50 percent of premature aging and early death is lifestyle-related. Translation: the decline that leads to decay is not predetermined. You can slow, halt, or even reverse many of its effects.

Biological aging is inevitable, but its slow pace is tied to the warning signs we've talked about. What makes it dangerous is its relentlessness. Nature never procrastinates. It never rests or takes a day off. But there's an unmerited benefit no one mentions— no one teaches it anywhere. You can match the force of biological aging. If you adopt a relentless routine, you not only can keep pace—you can beat it. Your growth can outpace decline.

With awareness, attention, and effort, you can become functionally younger. Arthritis, for example, is often seen as "just part of aging." But in reality, it's a disease of modern, sedentary living, compounded by excessive processed food and systemic inflammation. You could call it aging below the wrinkles. A poor lifestyle accelerates this aging.

Action and effort from you can halt or even reverse this decline. A 2017 article in *Physiological Reviews* put it bluntly:

"Physical inactivity is an underappreciated cause of almost all chronic diseases and conditions. Its outcome increases mortality and decreases healthspan. Remarkably, physical inactivity speeds biological aging."

In other words, poor lifestyle choices shorten lifespan and reduce our healthspan. And for all of us outdoor types on the path of aging, healthspan is everything.

Why We Age

Researchers have not yet pinned down a unified theory that explains why we age. Many say they cannot see a biological law that says we *must* age, and the upper limit of a long life of vitality is unknown. We do have scientific evidence that our biological systems —the ones that keep us spry, resilient, and carefree throughout much of our youth—begin to dull as we age.

This was evident to all of us during the 2020 coronavirus pandemic. Everyone was susceptible, but older adults suffered, were hospitalized, and died disproportionately. This was age-related decline in the robustness of immune systems, tragically animated in real time. Indeed, the dulling of our biological processes makes us more susceptible to disease as we age.

One key driver of decline is muscle loss. Almost every fly fisher and outdoor type I share this fact with is shocked to learn about the bodily changes that begin around middle age. Most people— even doctors—don't spend any time thinking about aging. They just treat the consequences.

But fly fishers and outdoor types do notice something is wrong. Perplexed by a body suddenly gone rogue, they ask for answers.

- "I haven't changed my diet, but I am getting rounder, doughier. It's as though my body is out of control, progressing downward on its own."
- "I've never had pain like this or been so stiff. Putting on my waders takes all my energy."
- "I do not have the balance and coordination I once had."
- "Backpacking used to be fun. Now it's too painful. I can't sleep on the ground."

One thing—the involuntary loss of muscle—drives these midlife changes. How can that be? Something so common that it happens to everyone walking the Earth is mostly unknown. Let's look at the changes in the body that occur as we age.

Hallmarks of Aging

Scientists have identified ten to twenty biological changes that occur in the aging human body upstream of disease, called the *hallmarks of aging*. Here are four we can most directly influence with lifestyle:

1. Involuntary loss of muscle—mitochondrial dysfunction and energy depletion
2. Chronic inflammation—drives chronic disease, pain, and suffering
3. Senescent cells—a "zombie" attack at the cellular level (*inflammaging*)
4. Reduced nicotinamide adenine dinucleotide (NAD) with a subsequent decline in sirtuin activity

Involuntary Loss of Muscle

We involuntarily lose muscle mass at a rate of 3–10 percent per decade after about age twenty-five, and this decline is progressive, increasing with each decade. This phenomenon poses the most critical threat to daily function. Posture, mobility, energy levels, and overall physiology are inextricably tied to muscle. The biggest threat to aging with strength and vigor is the loss of muscle, especially type-2 fast-twitch fibers—the ones that give us locomotion, strength, sturdiness, and coordination. For fly fishers and outdoor types, who demand more strength, more agility, and more stamina, muscle loss is unacceptable.

This process begins so gradually—and at such a small scale —that we don't notice it until it has progressed to stiffness and energy depletion. Muscle loss begins at the cellular level, and its effects show up in the quality and quantity of mitochondria, the tiny organelles that power our cells. For scale, one mito-chondrion is about 0.5 micrometer; a grain of salt is about 500 micrometers. That's the barely noticeable scale at which decline begins. The power of Nature is consistency: decline accumu-lates through incessant around-the-clock biological aging.

Mitochondria perform specialized functions as cellular pow-erhouses essential for energy production. Found in most cells, they are especially dense in energy-demanding organs such as the heart and eyes. These organs rely heavily on mitochondria to produce the energy required for their function. Thus, when we lose muscle, we lose energy. But there's no need to despair. Mito-chondria shrink in quality and quantity with years of physical in-activity, but this is reversible. When demand increases through exercise, they become larger and more numerous. A vigorous, long-term exercise habit can narrow many differences between young and older individuals. A journal article titled *Effects of Exercise on Mitochondrial Content and Function in Aging Human Skeletal Muscle*, published on the National Library of Medicine website, states: "Our main finding is that there is a robust improvement in skeletal muscle mitochondrial content and function in elderly men and women in response to an achievable program of moderate-intensity physical activity." This is one example of the human body's remarkable ability to heal, adapt, and reverse lifestyle-driven damage.

You can take back those car-to-office-to-couch years. Still, it's impossible to overstate the need to address muscle loss. Its detriments progress out of sight until, one day, a knee or an ankle gives out—or you fall, break a hip, or chip your elbow—and irreversible decline sets in. The CDC notes: "Falls among adults aged 65 and older are common, costly, and preventable."

A 2010 report in the journal *Clinical Nutrition and Metabolic Care* highlighted the seriousness, breadth, and depth of muscle loss: "The decrease in muscle mass is also accompanied by a progressive increase in fat mass and consequently changes in body composition and is associated with an increased incidence of insulin resistance in the elderly. Furthermore, bone density decreases, joint stiffness increases, and there is a small reduction in stature (kyphosis)." Muscle loss is more than mere dullness; it is a decline with deep and wide downstream vulnerabilities and implications. But you have agency—the power to end it, and even reverse it—right here and now.

Chronic Inflammation

As you may know, inflammation comes in two types. Acute inflammation is a natural healing response to injury, illness, or germs. It promotes healing and then subsides. Chronic inflammation, on the other hand, persists like an internal, smoldering fire, fueling cascading decline. When immune cells are triggered to respond to damage from internal or external stimuli, they secrete pro-inflammatory chemicals (cytokines) along with other signaling molecules. It's the body's reaction to "bad-actor" cells, removing them and initiating repair. But when this response becomes dysfunctional, it persists far beyond what benefits our health. Chronic inflammation damages tissue and contributes to diseases such as arthritis, high blood pressure, stroke, heart disease, asthma, diabetes, Alzheimer's, and cancer. Some researchers even call inflammation the root cause of all disease.

A 2024 article titled "Inflammation: The Cause of All Diseases," published in the journal *Cells*, concluded: "Chronic inflammation is linked to numerous diseases ('all diseases'), ranging from cardiovascular disease, type 2 diabetes, metabolic diseases, cancer, autoimmunity, gastrointestinal disorders, respiratory diseases, neurodegenerative diseases, reproductive system disorders, allergies, skin disorders, and joint problems to headaches, food sensitivities, hormonal imbalances, and sleep disorders." Clearly, reducing inflammation warrants our focused attention.

There are medical tests that measure inflammation, but unless you have a specific condition or medical need, they are generally not recommended—and insurance may not cover them.

A simple test you can do right now, standing in your own kitchen, is to ask and observe: Do you have pain-free mobility? If the answer is no, it may indicate that your muscles and joints are inflamed.

Too often, we accept muscle aches, body stiffness, and joint pain as unavoidable parts of getting older. This belief is outdated. Aging does not mean surrendering to pain. It is time to update both our thinking and our lifestyle.

Senescence

One major cause of chronic inflammation, especially as we age, is cellular senescence. It's when cells refuse to follow protocol. Senescent cells—cells that have stopped dividing but do not die —linger and accumulate in a half-alive state (often called *zombie cells*). They spew pro-inflammatory compounds that spread and "infect" healthy cells, creating an ever-expanding internal wildfire. Scientists now view chronic inflammation as an active process—a vicious cycle that contributes to premature aging. They've even coined a term for it: inflammaging.

You could earn the moniker *pre-inflamed* due to obesity, heart disease, type-2 diabetes, or inflammaging itself. A 2023 article in *Signal Transduction and Targeted Therapy* describes the process: "Factors secreted by senescent cells, known as the senescence-associated secretory phenotype (SASP), promote chronic inflammation and can induce senescence in normal cells. At the same time, chronic inflammation accelerates the senescence of immune cells, resulting in weakened immune function and an inability to clear senescent cells and inflammatory factors, which creates a vicious cycle of inflammation and senescence." This chronic inflammation—which increases the risk for age-related diseases, including organ damage—can be muted, reduced, and even reversed through our actions.

Nicotinamide Adenine Dinucleotide (NAD)

Please bear with me—this one isn't as difficult as it looks. I wouldn't burden you with biochemical names and processes if they weren't important for your health and longevity. All you need to remember is that NAD is a crucial coenzyme for over

500 chemical reactions in the body, and many of those reactions decline with age.

NAD works with signaling proteins at the apex of cellular activity. Sirtuins are a family of specialized signaling proteins that regulate survival, health, fitness, and the body's natural demolition, cleanup, recycling, healing, and infrastructure-building systems. They mute inflammation, boost mitochondrial production, and fight muscle loss. Sirtuins require the coenzyme NAD for activity. As we are learning, aging dampens NAD production, and sirtuin activity tapers.

This is yet another reason aging is so precarious. Scientists and aging researchers believe that reduced sirtuin/NAD activity is a major reason we become more susceptible to disease as we age. What will save us is awareness, attention, and effort. We must be keenly engaged as we get older.

A 2019 article in *Physiological Reports*—"Aerobic and Resistance Exercise Training Reverses Age-Dependent Decline in NAD+ Salvage Capacity in Human Skeletal Muscle"—described the benefits of exercise: "In the older individuals, exercise training was able to completely restore skeletal muscle NAMPT to levels observed in young individuals." (NAMPT, nicotinamide phosphoribosyltransferase, is an immediate precursor to NAD in the salvage pathway; the "+" in NAD+ denotes the oxidized form of NAD.)

Insight

Now that you have a grasp of what the threat of aging looks like, you have a better sense of why you cannot keep living as you did when you were younger. The spry resilience of the youthful human body is astonishing. It is slowed only by aging. Right about now, you might be asking, "Why isn't this life-changing information spread far and wide?" It's hard to say precisely.

Looking Back

When we look back, the early days of medicine hold some key pointers. The ancient Greek Hippocrates (460–375 BCE), widely acclaimed as the father of medicine, was also known as the first practitioner of the science of healthy lifestyle and disease prevention. His medical approach involved harmonizing the body and human physiology with Nature.

Food and nutrition were prioritized as fuel for optimal performance in the Olympic Games. Hippocrates also prioritized disease prevention and health building. His dictum: "Walking is man's best medicine. If we could give every individual the right amount of nourishment and exercise—not too little and not too much—we would have found the safest way to health." This "best way to health" approach was somehow lost and does not appear in modern medicine.

Current Climate

Our medical system is a business—a big business—and the connection to Nature has been replaced, or more like usurped, by pharmaceuticals. When you are sick, they make money. Building health may mean you rely less on their brightly lit, sanitized offices. That's not good for business. Modern nutrition is another behemoth industry not concerned with human performance. The standard American diet prioritizes profit over prevention, health, and longevity.

Our lineage and genetic makeup are a mismatch for today's world. Biological aging collides with modern, sedentary life. Add in nutrition and our modern medical system, and aging becomes a veritable train wreck.

Pause and reflect for a moment. Considering this context, are we 100 percent responsible for the current obesity rate and our frightening health crisis?

Upshift

Our bodies require more maintenance, care, and attention as we age. We simply must become active—an imperative supported by clinical evidence in a 2014 peer-reviewed article titled "Lack of Exercise Is a Major Cause of Chronic Diseases." This lengthy, eye-opening work reaches back three thousand years—before Hippocrates—and presents extensive evidence of a direct causal link between inactivity and avoidable chronic disease and decay. "A brief chronology of the three-millennia history that recognizes that physical inactivity reduces functional capacity and health; Cause vs. treatment are discussed to emphasize that physical inactivity is a primary cause of chronic conditions/diseases; Growing evidence that mechanisms by which inactivity causes disease differ from mechanisms by which physical activity is a therapy/treatment to act as a primary preventer of disease."

This paper is invaluable. It defines the different forms of exercise, explains what is meant by *functional capacity*, and clarifies the difference between activity and exercise. It is a thorough resource worth studying, reading, and rereading. This kind of deliberate reading differs from scanning for useful facts and bits of information; it is a deeper study. As you read and reflect, you'll be enkindled with awareness of past actions and habits that need updating—and how new behaviors will serve your current goals and desires far better.

This is the bedrock on which to build a new you. We cannot transform our medical system—our illness-care system—into authentic health care. This much-needed revolution will not arrive via a national campaign like the anti-smoking movement. It is an individual revolution. One by one, we will take control of our health and longevity—improving our healthspan.

Become the captain of your health, strength, and vigor. I follow the advice of the ancients, especially Hippocrates, though he lived more than two thousand years ago. He educated and empowered individuals to know and care for their bodies, admonishing his community, "If you are not your own doctor, you are a fool." A doctor will not give your aging systems the time, attention, and meticulous care they require and deserve. I am not saying we should shun medical professionals. I am saying: recognize your agency, become informed, and be your own advocate.

Exercise Is Medicine

Exercise as a preventive intervention provides benefits available nowhere else. No doctor, prescription, or supplement can offer what you can prescribe for yourself. Exercise can dramatically influence the trajectory of your health. It is well documented that through exercise you improve functional capacity and muscular strength, reduce chronic inflammation, increase HDL ("good") cholesterol, and lower body weight.

A 2019 article in *Sports Medicine and Health Science* reported "The implementation of daily physical activity and exercise prevention interventions support an 80% reduction in cardiovascular risk, 90% reduction in type 2 diabetes risk, 33% reduction in cancer risk, and in some cases reductions in all-cause mortality." You simply cannot get this kind of life-giving, proactive, preventive "medicine" anywhere except from your own efforts. You control the most potent health-giving care available to humans anywhere in the Universe.

Become your own doctor. Prescribe this medicine to yourself.

Exercise is effective because your body grows and thrives when in motion; conversely, it shuts down when motionless. In fact, you could say your biology becomes lazy and complacent with extended inactivity. Your systems are on constant alert, moment by moment, looking for signals to grow or to shut down. Lifestyle sends the signals that trigger your biology in either direction.

When you exercise, you connect with ancient biology—your lineage. Your body's response doesn't involve words or thought; it's all biology. *The American Journal of Lifestyle Medicine* puts it this way: "There is no medication treatment that can influence as many organ systems in a positive manner as can physical activity. Physical activity and associated improvements in physical fitness are key strategies to improving health."

What Doesn't Kill You

When you exercise, you create micro-stress in your muscles, causing tissue to break down at the cellular level. At the start of exercise, a complex, multisystem hormetic signal gears your cells, organs, and tissues to meet immediate energy demands. Chemicals and messenger proteins (cytokines—a type of myokine) secreted through muscle activity trigger growth hormone, insulin, testosterone, serotonin, adrenaline, and dozens of others to join the dance in your bloodstream. Exercise sends "grow" messages through cellular pathways.

Climbing stairs is a primordial act that doesn't involve thought—it's your ancient cellular biology at work. Your steps automatically send an "engage" message; your heart rate increases. Contracting muscles create increased demand that initiates this complex process, and oxygen, blood, and other chemicals are mobilized in harmony.

After exercise, you feel sore from the micro-breakdown of muscle cells. Here, a different set of complex messenger chemicals courses through your blood, initiating the pathways of repair and rebuild. This lasts for hours. Remember the 'no pain, no gain' cliché? Exercise breaks down muscle cells, and this micro-stress triggers the growth and repair-rebuild process.

We now know that the chemicals, proteins and hormones that heal, repair and rebuild infrastructure are not just for muscles. Your blood vessels, joints, bones, organs and brain all enjoy bathing in these repair and rebuild juices for several hours after exercising. You manipulate and direct this cellular 'growth/repair-rebuild biology' in your favor. And if you think about it, what could be more natural than using the body to repair, rebuild and heal the body? Exercise as if your life depends on it, because it does!

Hormesis is the scientific term for this natural micro-stress process. First described around 1880, researchers noticed that plants treated with diluted herbicide grew thicker. The mild stress triggered accelerated growth. Scientists were surprised. The light herbicide seemingly triggered a robust response. What mechanism caused this reaction? Are there similar mechanisms in other organisms?

Indeed, an ancient survival circuit was discovered to be prevalent in Nature. In humans, small doses of adversity or stress trigger survival-and-growth adaptation mechanisms. In response to micro-stress, you heal, become stronger, grow more resilient, and prepared biologically for the next—perhaps more critical—stressor. Hormesis is adaptive micro-trauma. Sometimes called "longevity pathways" or "survival circuits," these mechanisms maintain and restore vitality.

The biological processes that decline with age awaken in response to hormetic actions. The body becomes resilient once again—to more youthful levels. Thus, what doesn't kill you makes you stronger.

Daily exercise triggers hormesis, which stimulates growth, longevity, and survival pathways. As muscle grows, NAD is stimulated to grow; sirtuins activate, reducing inflammation and stimulating the natural demolition, recycling, and cleanup of old, tired cells. Mitochondria grow in number and improve in function.

Remember, mitochondria are the body's energy source. They convert food and oxygen into energy in the form of adenosine triphosphate (ATP), short-term biological "batteries" that power cellular processes. ATP is especially abundant in the heart, brain, and muscles—energy-intensive systems.

That is why it is so important to stimulate the body's hormetic response: you reawaken and boost critical energy systems. Researchers writing in *Dose-Response* call it mitochondrial hormesis or mitohormesis and they wrote, "One of the main changes due to regular physical activity is the increase in mitochondria energy metabolism."

It doesn't take much exercise to reawaken and boost these systems and release growth hormone, testosterone, insulin, adrenaline, and healing factors into your bloodstream. You literally amp up energy production, inducing muscles to grow new infrastructure (capillaries) to meet increased demand for blood and oxygen.

The body responds dramatically to physical stressors like exercise (the best-understood hormetic strategy). Functional-medicine physicians everywhere agree. Chronic stress has a negative impact on the body, but small acute stressors are strategic actions that will positively influence your health and longevity.

Paying attention to hormesis teaches us about human biology. Nature is not static or routine; it's active, responsive, intuitive, and dynamic. When you stimulate your body through hormetic strategies, you reconnect with ancient biological pathways on a profoundly deep and personal level—you are collaborating on a primal level with Nature.

Researchers have identified about twenty longevity genes, all triggered by hormetic strategies. It's a beautiful system: biological processes decline with age but can be reawakened and stimulated toward youthful levels through effort. We apply the body's natural medicine—our innate healing processes—where the only side effect is more energy and better health.

Fasting

That same hormetic intelligence senses and responds to nutrients. Through cellular pathways, it senses when and what you are eating with exquisite detail and harmony. We know some of the mechanisms, but the system is so complex, dynamic, and multifaceted that its totality is unknowable.

Fasting is in our lineage; we evolved with scarcity. Imagine it's dusk and your small group of hunter-gatherers is running down an antelope. In the last seconds, it gets away. You are hungry. On this day, protein is scarce. Automatically, hormesis is triggered: your body goes into survival mode, and built-in defenses are released. Scarcity triggers survival. We cannot say that about abundance.

Today, fasting or time-restricted eating mimics ancestral patterns and reconnects you with primordial biology by triggering hormesis through the same endowed survival pathways. Though fasting or calorie restriction may appear passive, it is an active approach to hormesis and considered the holy grail of longevity. But you do not have to starve yourself. Chemists, researchers, and biologists are exploring ways to mimic distress-free calorie restriction, recognizing that feeling hungry isn't something most people seek out. Fortunately, there are as many ways to fast as there are people. Perhaps the easiest is taking advantage of sleep.

Avoid eating upon waking; hold off on breakfast for a few hours. It's best to wait at least twelve hours. Have an early dinner, sleep normally, and don't eat until twelve hours have passed. It's not difficult—this way, you mimic starvation without starving. Over time, you may find it easy to extend to thirteen, fourteen, sixteen, or eighteen hours. Some people condition themselves to fast for an entire day. This induces the natural "trash pickup" process of autophagy ("self-eating"), in which cells recycle and renew.

The body switches to survival mode, scavenging weak or inactive senescent cells—Pac-Man-style—to meet energy needs. This critical cleanup absorbs old, damaging cells and works to reduce inflammation.

The consensus among scientists and aging researchers is that modern life is imbalanced: not enough autophagy and far too much caloric influx, forcing constant digestion. A steady fifty to sixty years of non-stop food influx promotes lazy, complacent biology. Constant calories signal, "Times are good; turn off survival pathways." Not enough cellular cleanup, repair, and healing allows a buildup of senescent (zombie) cells and proteins—and possibly pollutants such as plastics and other contaminants. Fasting is your break from the continuous demands of digestion, an important step toward longevity.

Hormesis can also be induced through cold plunges and saunas, resistance training, and high-intensity interval training (HIIT). These require some personal risk, experimentation, and self-education. You must determine your fitness level and what is right for you.

Cold plunges can shock the body. Resistance training is specialized; to avoid injury, consider hiring a personal trainer. HIIT requires a solid baseline aerobic capacity; at minimum, a treadmill stress test from a medical professional is a required prerequisite.

Nutrition Pathways

In addition to fasting, another exciting way to harness mild hormetic stress is through nutritional pathways. The human body possesses complex, highly sensitive nutrient-sensing systems. Your biology never sleeps—it is constantly rebuilding, rewiring, adapting, and healing. It incessantly looks for triggers, messages, and coded cellular instructions—what hormone, coenzyme, or pathway to turn on—based on input from you. Your body reacts to every morsel you ingest.

You've likely heard that a plant-based diet is highly beneficial. Science is only beginning to unlock the power of plants to prevent disease and extend life. Certain plants contain natural toxins designed to deter insects, herbivores, and other pests. In humans, the levels of these toxins are low enough to mimic a mild, beneficial hormetic stress. When you hear that a food is "good for you," it likely contains a toxin or antioxidant property that leads to a hormetic response— cellular healing or rebuilding.

A new family of compounds—senolytics—shows promise in targeting zombie cells. A 2020 report in the *Journal of Internal Medicine* concluded that "Senolytics appear to delay, prevent, or alleviate multiple age-related conditions and chronic diseases and enhance healthspan and lifespan in experimental animals," suggesting potential interventions for humans to delay, prevent, or treat senescence and age-related conditions. In other words, the right foods are medicine. Because senescence is a hallmark of aging, living with a high number of these zombies pushes the balance toward inflammation and premature aging. Simply eating more plants can put you on the path to becoming functionally younger.

Senolytics include fisetin (strawberries, apples, cucumbers, onions); luteolin (carrots, broccoli, artichokes, onions, cabbages, berries, citrus fruits, cherries, blueberries, apples, kale); quercetin (citrus fruits, apples, berries, onions); and curcumin (turmeric). This is a start, far from an exhaustive list.

Whole foods are always best, but many of these phytonutrients are also sold as supplements. Be cautious and well-informed with supplements. Many are marketed cleverly alongside drugs that make FDA-approved treatment claims and disclose side effects. Read carefully: slick marketing can persuade consumers that all supplements are safe and approved.

The power contained within plants cannot be overstated. Age-reversing, longevity-building phytonutrients show so much potential as medicines of the future that the Rockefeller Foundation is spearheading the Periodic Table of Food Initiative (PTFI) to map biomolecules that occur in plants.

More than 26,000 biomolecules occur in plants, the overwhelming majority of which are unidentified and whose health effects are generally unknown. The near-term goal of the PTFI is to begin filling the black hole of nutritional knowledge by uncovering the biomolecular composition of foods through a global network of collaborators provided with standardized tools and training.

Working with top research labs on each continent and partnering with a growing network of national lab hubs, PTFI aims to translate food science for all regional landscapes and traditional diets.

The longer-term goal is to create an equity-centered, evidence-based system to prevent or treat diet-triggered diseases.

Imagine a doctor's visit in 2030.

After evaluating your health, your doctor makes diet recommendations far more specific than "eat your greens." Is Butter lettuce better for your symptoms than Romaine? Should you add cherry tomatoes or Roma? Eat a Gaia apple or a Granny Smith?

Healthcare providers can offer this advice because they understand both food composition and food/body interactions down to the molecular level, thanks to the contributions of researchers and scientists.

Now imagine 2050.

Nutrition is deeply personalized and aimed at preventing illnesses or resolving them before symptoms appear. You scan individual food items to determine whether they will support your health needs.

Your Body, the Ecosystem

My work as a wildlife biologist centered on habitat—evaluating and, when necessary, restoring wetlands, salt marshes, forests, and prairies to ensure their health and integrity. The health of each habitat contributes upward to the wellness of the larger ecosystem—the entire community of living things. Healthy ecosystems are naturally resilient. When they have baseline vigor, they intrinsically bounce back from a setback like a storm, flood, drought, or die-off. Ecosystem resilience is a natural quality determined by the integrity of its parts.

The slightest weakness in a habitat creates an opening for disease or other threats. Forests stressed by drought are an open door to beetle infestations, blight, or fungal attack. Polluted or drained wetlands are weakened and more susceptible to decline, invasions of exotic species, and other disruptions.

That's how Nature works. Humans are no different. Your body is an ecosystem. The "habitats" that contribute to a healthy human ecosystem include your muscles, tendons, organ systems, nervous system, gut, and many others. Building health must focus on maintaining and improving processes, not treating symptoms.

Popping a few acetaminophen tablets may provide temporary symptom relief. Addressing the root cause, however, requires a long-term, lifestyle and/or systemic approach. It is not a quick-fix, suppress-the-symptoms affair. Degraded ecosystems are repaired with a long-term restorative approach: we address root-level problems and reinvigorate natural processes that return ecosystems to their innate, self-sustaining resilience.

Input

Everything you think, every morsel you eat, and what you drink and do—or don't do—influence what goes on in your body. The products of your lifestyle are present in your blood, continually shaping your physiology. Metabolites (products of metabolism), hormones, proteins, catalysts, insulin, coenzymes, and a host of other chemicals course through every curve of your body. This chemical bath is the literal lifeblood of your internal ecosystem.

You've probably grasped the obvious: life-giving ecosystems are balanced. Not too much acid or too much base. Plenty of whole food. Not too much sugar, flour, or ultra-processed (predigested) food. Much like garden soil, plants will not thrive without life-supporting amounts of compost, nutrients, and loam. Like any ecosystem, nothing happens in isolation; one chemical or substance influences the expression of another. All organisms (humans included) thrive in a healthy ecosystem. The opposite is also true: there are ingredients to health and impediments to health.

Our modern diet is drastically low in fiber and dense in calories, to our detriment. The human microbiome in our gut creates metabolites from what we eat. Without fiber to feed on, our microbiome cannot create the healthy metabolites we need to thrive—that gives space for less healthy (sometimes invasive) microbes to grow.

Build Health From the Gut Outward

Even though Hippocrates supposedly said "All disease begins in the gut" more than two thousand years ago, we are only beginning to take notice. Scientists now recognize that gut health—the diversity of our microbiome—is the epicenter of immunity, metabolism, and inflammation. Indeed, 70 to 80 percent of immune cells are found in the gut. The twist is that we rely on nonhuman species to build immunity, reduce inflammation, and build health. The microbes living in our gut are so numerous and diverse that they form a mini-ecosystem within our larger bodily ecosystem. A report in *BioMed Research International* puts the number in the trillions: "The gut is the most colonized human organ, with up to 100 trillion microbes—about ten times the number of human cells."

The more diverse, unprocessed whole foods you eat, the richer, more diverse, and more life-supporting your microbiome becomes. When you hear that blueberries, onions, mushrooms, and apples are good for your brain or heart, what is actually being said is that these foods are good for your microbiome. Whole, natural, nutrient-rich, high-fiber foods light up your microbiome, allowing full synthesis and absorption.

It is critically important to become literate and keenly engaged in how your lifestyle choices influence your physiology. Recognize the highly impactful role of nutrition. A healthy microbiome is flooded with unprocessed, undigested or partially digested, diverse, high-fiber foods—mostly from plants. Individual microbial species transform that potential energy into metabolites—molecules that signal and trigger healing, immune, and anti-inflammatory responses. As an article in *Molecular Metabolism* titled "A Healthy Gastrointestinal Microbiome Is Dependent on Dietary Diversity" notes, "Like all healthy ecosystems, richness of microbiota species characterizes the GI microbiome in healthy individuals. Conversely, a loss in species diversity is a common finding in several disease states." This spells out, in no uncertain terms, the control we have over our health.

Indeed, microbial metabolism produces products that can serve or subvert health: "In a healthy state, gut microbiota metabolites are helpful for maintaining the basic functions of hosts, whereas disturbed production of these metabolites can lead to numerous diseases such as cardiovascular diseases, gastrointestinal diseases, neurodegenerative diseases, and cancer." Even a mild disruption to metabolism can hinder the body's ability to break down what we eat for energy.

This miraculously complex symbiotic relationship, which provides life-giving metabolites that build immunity and health, is not fully understood. We recognize the importance of gut microbiota, but "The number of them is so huge that many remain uncharacterized."

We don't have to know how everything works to live better and longer. It is enough to grasp the impact—to know that an estimated one-third to one-half of our metabolites come from gut bacteria. We can improve gut health by eating a wide array of plant-derived whole foods. Whole foods promote anti-inflammatory microbes, while the standard American diet promotes pro-inflammatory, pathogenic (disease-causing) microbe growth.

There is an important bonus: the healthier your microbiome, the more calories it will absorb—and the fewer calories you will absorb.

In a report in *Nutrients*, researchers found a causal connection between high sugar intake and pro-inflammatory gut microbiota. Overly processed, sugar-laden meals may fill you up but they stagger the balance of microbiota to the pathogen side. "The so-called Western diet is rich in saturated fat and sugars and poor in plant-derived fibers, and it is associated with an increased risk of metabolic and cardiovascular diseases, as well as chronic (low-grade) inflammation." It is well known that a high-sugar diet creates a pro-inflammatory internal environment that disrupts gut microbiota.

Less well known: when you improve the environment in

which inflammation, chronic pain, stiffness, or disease exists, you build health systemically—and conditions often improve dramatically. You read that right. When you create health, disease fades. Use the body to heal the body. Nature supersedes medicine.

Three Tactics

Three mutually advantageous tactics—exercise, fasting, and nutrition—work in concert. You'll increase endurance and build muscle, offsetting losses from biological aging, and serve yourself on multiple levels from the inside out.

Better awareness of nutritional choices, coupled with fasting, is a two-pronged effort. Reducing inflammation and feeding an increasingly diverse microbiome will cool inflammation and trigger autophagy, the body's natural cleanup and recycling crew. An intrinsic part of nutrition is hydration. One study linked it to longevity. It is critical for energy, joint health and pliability (synovial fluid in your joints is mostly water). Explore other options than sugar-laden drinks as sugar is associated with inflammation.

These three actions are a literal road to improvement. But they take uncommon commitment, effort, and patience. Remember, we are creating improvement at the cellular level. It takes time for a condition to manifest, and healing begins at the cellular level as well. Trust your miraculous body to work for you in ways you will feel over time.

Your Life is Your Message

You can begin exercising at any age. In fact, many people come to it later in life. Results come at any age. The last decades of your life could be the most significant. You have amassed the wisdom, skill, and patience to mentor and influence. You now offer tremendous value in helping perpetuate the legacy of fly-fishing.

If you can show up in the best health possible—free of anxiety, dread, and pain; engaged, caring, and involved—you will be a compelling model for the rest of us. Let's look at how exercise can help.

Exercise

Developing aerobic endurance will make your heart stronger. You will build the stamina to wade and fly-fish with vigor—not just for longer days but for a lifetime. Once you have a solid foundation of aerobic capacity, strength, and coordination, you can tune up fine-motor skills with balance and stability work. Your body will transform into a strong, sturdy, enviable frame.

Exercising in specific ways will "turn on" pathways of growth. Long, slow aerobic work uses your type-1 muscles, requires copious oxygen, and increases circulation. You build endurance—the ability to sustain low-level exertion over extended periods. If you can walk briskly or jog for forty-five minutes to an hour, imagine the stamina you'll bring to your fly-fishing.

Endurance training burns fat and invigorates your immune system. It is health-building work that enables healing. Numerous studies report that as heart health goes up; biological aging goes down. Endurance training is foundational for every Olympic hopeful and Tour de France athlete. It's also a necessity for fly fishers who hike into blue lines far from parking areas and wade cold streams full of slippery rocks. You're in good company.

Endurance Training

Jog, walk, row, run, ruck, swim, or bike at a moderate 60–65 percent of maximum heart rate (MHR). MHR is 220 minus your age. For a fifty-year-old, MHR ≈ 170; 65 percent ≈ 110 beats per minute. Use a heart rate monitor or the "talk test." You can converse, but only in short sentences because you're breathing harder.

The ideal is to raise your heart rate to 60–65 percent of MHR and keep it there for forty-five minutes to one hour. In the beginning, do what you can. If you can manage only 15 minutes at ~40 percent of max heart rate, do that. If your heart rate spikes, slow down, walk, or call it a day. Then do it again tomorrow. Endurance is built through consistent effort. Next week, do a bit more—maybe twenty minutes.

If fifteen minutes is your absolute maximum, do that—every day, for the rest of your life. Do what you can. The greatest benefit comes from the doing. Connect with your body and watch your fly-fishing transform.

Consistent aerobic exercise over months and years will dramatically improve your circulatory system. You may grow new capillaries to meet muscles' demand for blood and oxygen. You will certainly influence the day-to-day expression of your DNA. Remember: as heart health rises, biological aging falls. You can become functionally younger.

If you stay with the effort long-term, you'll build a bigger engine. Then you can shift to building aerobic capacity—VO_2 max —by adding interval training. VO_2 max is your maximum rate of oxygen use during sprint-type efforts; it reflects overall cardiovascular fitness and is sometimes used to predict longevity.

Sprinting—short bursts of speed and elevated effort—pushes your heart rate beyond 65 percent. The upper target is about 85 percent of MHR. At this level you burn more glucose. Mitochondria are magical. They can burn fat or glucose depending on which pathway is stimulated. During intervals (high-intensity interval training, or HIIT) fat still burns in the background, but you've added "racing fuel" and created a metabolic upshift. Intervals induce pathways that not only burn glucose but also release human growth hormone (HGH) and other growth-related compounds. Higher intensity improves fitness faster—but use extreme caution. HIIT requires a robust aerobic base before you begin.

If you are just beginning, you could reach your target of 85 percent MHR by walking fast. Heart rate is the trigger. That's what matters. You don't have to pound the ground. Walking, biking or stair-stepping—the focus is on heart rate using any mechanism.

Before starting any program—especially intervals—get medical clearance. At a minimum, ask your doctor for a treadmill stress test. I had my first at age forty and repeat the investment every four or five years.

Resistance Training

I recommend a trainer for resistance, strength, or weight training because it's more specialized. Unlike aerobic training, where you recover overnight, resistance work needs about a 48-hour repair/ rebuild cycle. Two days per week is adequate; three is the maximum. You must learn to break down muscles safely—exhausting them without overloading them or damaging joints. Strong muscles can stress joints. When this happens (often), people self-diagnose "weak joints." Not so—joints simply receive far less blood flow than muscles and heal more slowly.

Resistance training is serious business—you get one body. If you go too hard, with too much weight too soon, injury will sideline you. Specific movements, patience, and care are required to strengthen ligaments and tendons that support the muscles you're building. Knowledge, finesse, and extra-careful time and attention will help you grow pain- and injury-free.

I treat joints and back as sensitive and easily strained. Go slow and be methodical. Less weight—even just body weight— is best at the start. Limber, pain-free range of motion matters more than how much weight you can move.

We're not chasing beach muscles. We're building functional strength to support an arduous fly-fishing life.

If you're sidelined, your focus shifts to healing and returning. Setbacks hurt because the older you are, the longer healing takes. You need every workout to be a contribution—a building block. Consistency beats intensity.

You can do resistance training every day if you split sessions. Try chest/shoulders/triceps one day and legs/back/biceps the next—it's important to learn the different muscles and program accordingly.

Beginning on your own is fine—for a while. Start with body-weight work. Then hire a trainer. A trainer will dial in technique, form, and routine quickly. It won't cost as much as a good fly rod, and most trainers would love to hear, "I want to get in condition for hardcore fly-fishing—can you help me with resistance training?" They'll answer your fitness questions better than any app.

For an overall strategy, work the large muscle groups to maximize engagement of growth pathways: chest (push-ups, bench press); back (chin-ups, deadlifts, rows); quads (squats, leg press). Use only body weight until you have sound form and a baseline of strength—or until your trainer advances you.

Resistance training brings extensive benefits. Coordination improves alongside strength, and conditioned muscle is metabolically active—it confers advantages to non-muscle tissues, too. You may not be able to name every benefit, but you'll feel them.

A little-known miraculous fact about muscle: the more you have, the better—especially for staving off disease, including cancer. A 2021 report in the *British Medical Bulletin* found, "Resistance training and other exercises are the best strategy available to maintain or increase muscle mass and are recommended in most national statements on exercise for cancer care. The larger the muscle mass of the patient, the greater the production of anti-cancer molecules, and this muscle mass should be activated frequently, preferably daily, at an intensity sufficient to dose the cancer with this 'exercise medicine.'" Exercise is medicine—and you prescribe it.

Chronic Illness

Chronic illness is a reality for many of us. According to the Centers for Disease Control and Prevention (CDC), nearly half of adults in the U.S. live with at least one chronic condition. Don't let a diagnosis prevent progress. The presence of one or more chronic conditions is not a reason to avoid exercise —it's a reason to lean in and exercise wisely and vigorously. The clinical evidence is overwhelming. Don't allow illness to sideline you from the most potent antidote. Get your clinician's approval—and train like your life depends on it, because it does.

Stability and Stretching

Stability and balance training will refine the motor skills in the muscle you build—you literally enhance connections between muscles and the nervous system. Don't overlook yoga. It builds strength, flexibility, stamina, and balance; as a practice, it enhances every corner of life.

Stretch from head to toe as part of daily conditioning. If you can't do the classic sit-and-reach, don't despair—it's hard, because it stretches hamstrings and lower back at once. Try a single-leg sit-and-reach or use a chair. Movement is the key. Stretch to your current ability and build from there. With consistency, the sit-and-reach becomes easy. Flexibility comes with practice—just like everything else.

Do Something Every Day

If this sounds like a lot, you're right. Living with strength and vitality—and longevity as a goal—is not free. As with a weed-free, productive garden, daily attention is required. How do you want your life to be—directed by the tide of aging, doctors, and pharmaceuticals, or directed by you and Nature?

You have control.

You are an experiment of one. Try things. Learn how much control you have. Use this guide as a framework. Listen to your body. Build your own routine to blunt decline and disease. Use each day to build health.

Be patient; give yourself time to adjust. Unfold the new you slowly. You can find countless exercises online. You are in control. Remember: effort is the only requirement—progress, not perfection.

You will grow. Nothing can guarantee more days in your life, but you will stack the deck in your favor. More life to your days is a certainty—more life to your fly-fishing days.

A Powerful Mental Trick

Olympic athletes know that performance requires mental and physical training. It takes deliberate intention to stay focused and committed. But know that physical and mental strength grow in parallel.

Researchers have shown that neither 100 percent pessimism nor 100 percent optimism is most effective for success. History shows that people who find the "sweet spot" between the two fare best—even in the worst circumstances (prisoners of war, in concentration camps, or in solitary confinement).

The trick: remain optimistic while accepting present difficulty. Invest in the work—exercise, fasting, and optimal nutrition—like a pessimist, while keeping the dream in focus like an optimist (a long life of hardcore fly-fishing).

Total optimists often crumble under extreme conditions (think Navy SEAL training). But a balance works: "I know I'm going to get old" (pessimism). And "I'm excited to take control of my aging to stay vigorous" (optimism). You could call it realistic optimism.

One More Cast

You came to this book because a part of you refuses to trade wild water for waiting rooms. To you, senior living means slinging a fly rod, shouldering a pack, stepping into cold current, and casting in roadless places. What matters now are more dawns, more rises, and more bends in the river.

Nature has given you agency in how your story plays out. Your body responds to attention the way a river responds to rain—quietly at first, then with unmistakable strength.

What we've learned together is simple, if not always easy. Aging is not a verdict; it is life giving you warning signs. Pain, stiffness, softening strength, flagging energy, poor balance, and trouble staying warm—nothing is punishing you. This is a heads up. All of it will respond to your input.

- Muscle wanes when it is not used.
- Mitochondria shrink when they are not asked to work.
- Chronic inflammation smolders when we sit and when our food is engineered for shelf life rather than for life.
- Senescent cells linger when cleanup systems idle.

- NAD declines until triggered to grow.
- Microbiome—the small nation that lives within us—either builds or blunts immunity depending on what we feed it.

Do not wait for perfect conditions. There is no perfect day, only the day you have. Trade drift for direction and add life to your days, and then—almost by accident—you may find there are more days, too.

Aging also requires a change in posture—mental as much as physical. Train like a pessimist—consistent, meticulous, no shortcuts. Dream like an optimist—seeing yourself at eighty or ninety stepping confidently across slick rocks, reading water with the wisdom that only miles confer.

Make this a promise to yourself and to those who watch what you do more than what you say:

- Move every day.
- Lift with care, twice or thrice a week.
- Eat real food, lots of plants; give digestion a rest.
- Sleep on schedule; enjoy Nature often.
- Practice balance—in the gym, on the trail, in your head.
- Teach what you learn to the next angler you meet who thinks age has the final word.
- Keep your humor.

This is not a doctrine; it is a habitat-restoration plan for the aging human ecosystem. You enhance processes, and symptoms fade. Restore the river; trout return.

Thank you for reading this guide. I invite you to learn more and join our newsletter group.

Stay Well!

Brian Braudis, brian@flyfisherfitness.com

About the Author

Brian Braudis has a congenital draw to Nature. His first steps were chasing birds and, by age seven, trailing them to hidden nests, studying biology—from hatchling to fledge. He spent countless hours immersed with insects in jars, chipmunks in box traps, chub minnows in streams, snakes, toads, and darting salamanders under logs.

At a Cub Scout outing, he saw his first fly fisher. Mesmerized by the mastery and grace of each cast, he knew instantly: someday, he would be there.

A sudden tragedy altered his course. When his father died of a heart attack at fifty-three, Brian set aside boyhood dreams of fly-fishing and shifted to survival.

Through a series of steps, missteps, serendipity and good fortune, Brian earned a biology degree and was hired as a wildlife biologist and later served in a leadership role with the U.S. Fish and Wildlife Service. Inherent aptitude became interwoven with vocation.

With his passion for Nature met, he focused his spare time on family and a devotion to fitness.

After retirement, fly-fishing with vigor, avoiding premature aging, building health, and longevity became Brian's purpose.

The Ageless Angler came about through a two-stage journey. Brian educated himself about the biological laziness that ensues with modern life and used experimentation to stimulate the body out of laziness and complacency, pushing it to grow, thrive and supplant disease.

The good news is that the fraction of time and effort invested in this journey will give you an entire lifetime of strength and vitality.

Notes

A Word on Genetics

Passarino G, De Rango F, Montesanto A. Human longevity: Genetics or Lifestyle? It takes two to tango. Immun Ageing. 2016 Apr 5;13:12. doi: 10.1186/s12979-016-0066-z. PMID: 27053941; PMCID: PMC4822264.

Biological Age

https://www.prb.org/resources/up-to-half-of-u-s-premature-deaths-are-preventable-behavioral-factors-key/

https://pmc.ncbi.nlm.nih.gov/articles/PMC6347102/ Role of Inactivity and Chronic Disease

Hallmarks of Aging

https://www.cell.com/cell/pdf/S0092-8674(22)01377-0.pdf

• **Involuntary Loss of Muscle**

Johnson ML, Robinson MM, Nair KS. Skeletal muscle aging and the mitochondrion. Trends Endocrinol Metab. 2013

May;24(5):247-56. doi: 10.1016/j.tem.2012.12.003. Epub 2013 Feb 1. PMID: 23375520; PMCID: PMC3641176.

Menshikova EV, Ritov VB, Fairfull L, Ferrell RE, Kelley DE, Goodpaster BH. Effects of exercise on mitochondrial content and function in aging human skeletal muscle. J Gerontol A Biol Sci Med Sci. 2006 Jun;61(6):534-40. doi: 10.1093/gerona/61.6.534. PMID: 16799133; PMCID: PMC1540458.

https://www.cdc.gov/mmwr/volumes/72/wr/mm7235a1.htm

Volpi E, Nazemi R, Fujita S. Muscle tissue changes with aging. Curr Opin Clin Nutr Metab Care. 2004 Jul;7(4):405-10. doi: 10.1097/01.mco.0000134362.76653.b2. PMID: 15192443; PMCID: PMC2804956.

• **Chronic Inflammation**

https://www.mdpi.com/2073-4409/13/22/1906

• **Senescence**

https://www.nature.com/articles/s41392-023-01502-8

• **Nicotinamide Adenine Dinucleotide (NAD)**

de Guia RM, Agerholm M, Nielsen TS, Consitt LA, Søgaard D, Helge JW, Larsen S, Brandauer J, Houmard JA, Treebak JT. Aerobic and resistance exercise training reverses age-dependent decline in NAD+ salvage capacity in human skeletal muscle. Physiol Rep. 2019 Jul;7(12):e14139. doi: 10.14814/phy2.14139. PMID: 31207144; PMCID: PMC6577427.

Upshift

Booth FW, Roberts CK, Laye MJ. Lack of exercise is a major cause of chronic diseases. Compr Physiol. 2012 Apr;2(2):1143-211. doi: 10.1002/cphy.c110025. PMID: 23798298; PMCID: PMC4241367.

Exercise is Medicine

Anderson E, Durstine JL. Physical activity, exercise, and chronic diseases: A brief review. Sports Med Health Sci. 2019 Sep 10;1(1):3-10. doi: 10.1016/j.smhs.2019.08.006. PMID: 35782456; PMCID: PMC9219321.

Thompson WR, Sallis R, Joy E, Jaworski CA, Stuhr RM, Trilk JL. Exercise Is Medicine. Am J Lifestyle Med. 2020 Apr 22;14(5):511-523. doi: 10.1177/1559827620912192. PMID: 32922236; PMCID: PMC7444006.

What Doesn't Kill You

Wan, Y., Liu, J., Mai, Y. et al. Current advances and future trends of hormesis in disease. npj Aging 10, 26 (2024). https://doi.org/10.1038/s41514-024-00155-3

Ristow M, Schmeisser K. Mitohormesis: Promoting Health and Lifespan by Increased Levels of Reactive Oxygen Species (ROS). Dose Response. 2014 Jan 31;12(2):288-341. doi: 10.2203/dose-response.13-035.Ristow. PMID: 24910588; PM-CID: PMC4036400.

Nutrition Pathways

Kirkland JL, Tchkonia T. Senolytic drugs: from discovery to translation. J Intern Med. 2020 Nov;288(5):518-536. doi: 10.1111/joim.13141. Epub 2020 Aug 4. PMID: 32686219; PMCID: PMC7405395.

https://www.rockefellerfoundation.org/initiatives/periodic-table-of-food/

Build Health from the Gut Outward

Rizzatti G, Lopetuso LR, Gibiino G, Binda C, Gasbarrini A. Proteobacteria: A Common Factor in Human Diseases. Biomed Res Int. 2017;2017:9351507. doi: 10.1155/2017/9351507. Epub 2017 Nov 2. PMID: 29230419; PMCID: PMC5688358.

Heiman ML, Greenway FL. A healthy gastrointestinal microbiome is dependent on dietary diversity. Mol Metab. 2016 Mar 5;5(5):317-320. doi: 10.1016/j.molmet.2016.02.005. PMID: 27110483; PMCID: PMC4837298.

Liu J, Tan Y, Cheng H, Zhang D, Feng W, Peng C. Functions of Gut Microbiota Metabolites, Current Status and Future Perspectives. Aging Dis. 2022 Jul 11;13(4):1106-1126. doi: 10.14336/AD.2022.0104. PMID: 35855347; PMCID: PMC 9286904.

Liu J, Tan Y, Cheng H, Zhang D, Feng W, Peng C. Functions of Gut Microbiota Metabolites, Current Status and Future Perspectives. Aging Dis. 2022 Jul 11;13(4):1106-1126. doi:

10.14336/AD.2022.0104. PMID: 35855347; PMCID: PMC 9286904.

Satokari R. High Intake of Sugar and the Balance between Pro- and Anti-Inflammatory Gut Bacteria. Nutrients. 2020 May 8;12(5):1348. doi: 10.3390/nu12051348. PMID: 32397233; PMCID: PMC7284805.

Three Tactics

https://www.nih.gov/news-events/nih-research-matters/link-between-hydration-aging

Your Life is Your Message

https://www.deseret.com/2024/1/22/24047117/93-year-old-indoor-rowing-champion/

Exercise

https://www.theguardian.com/science/2023/nov/06/scientists-name-eight-measures-that-can-slow-ageing-by-up-to-six-years

Resistance Training

Thomas R, Kenfield SA, Yanagisawa Y, Newton RU. Why exercise has a crucial role in cancer prevention, risk reduction and improved outcomes. Br Med Bull. 2021 Sep 10;139(1):100-119. doi: 10.1093/bmb/ldab019. PMID: 34426823; PMCID: PMC8431973

Chronic Illness

https://www.cdc.gov/pcd/issues/2024/23_0267.htm

A Powerful Mental Trick

https://www.psychologytoday.com/gb/blog/the-athletes-way/202007/one-more-reason-rethink-the-power-positive-thinking

www.ingramcontent.com/pod-product-compliance
Lightning Source LLC
Chambersburg PA
CBHW070800050426
42452CB00012B/2415